THE ART OF MINDFUL ORIGAMI

ABOUT THE AUTHOR

Dr Richard Chambers is a clinical psychologist and internationally recognized expert in mindfulness. He has published two previous books, *Mindful Learning* and *Mindful Relationships*, and numerous journal articles. He is regularly interviewed by mainstream media and consults for a growing number of businesses, sports clubs, healthcare organizations and educational institutions. Richard is spearheading a world-first, university-wide mindfulness initiative at Monash University in Melbourne, Australia. He is also one of the developers of Smiling Mind, a free mindfulness app with over a million downloads.

THE ART OF MINDFUL ORIGAMI

SOOTHE THE MIND WITH 15 BEAUTIFUL
ORIGAMI PROJECTS AND ACCOMPANYING
MINDFULNESS EXERCISES

DR RICHARD CHAMBERS

EXISLE
PUBLISHING

First published 2016

Exisle Publishing Pty Ltd
'Moonrising', Narone Creek Road, Wollombi,
NSW 2325, Australia

P.O. Box 60–490, Titirangi,
Auckland 0642, New Zealand
www.exislepublishing.com

A CiP record for this book is available from the
National Library of Australia.

ISBN 978-1-925335-29-3

Designed by Sarah Anderson
Typeset in Futura
Printed in China

This book uses paper sourced under ISO 14001 guidelines from well-managed
forests and other controlled sources.

10 9 8 7 6 5 4 3 2 1

Photo credits
Copyright © in photographs and images as listed below:
Photographs of completed origami projects by Sarah Anderson
Instructional diagrams by Sarah Anderson
Origami and colouring-in papers courtesy of Shutterstock

THIS BOOK IS DEDICATED TO
MY TEACHERS AND TO ALL THE
ACTIVITIES THAT INVITE US INTO
FULLY EXPERIENCING THE MOMENT.

CONTENTS

GIFT BOX **14**

DRINKING CUP **17**

SAIL BOAT **20**

CRANE **23**

STAR **26**

PINWHEEL **29**

SAMURAI HELMET **33**

HEART **35**

FOX **38**

PUPPY FACE **41**

BUTTERFLY **44**

JUMPING FROG **47**

PINE TREE **50**

LOTUS **53**

BOW **56**

BEFORE YOU FOLD

THE HISTORY OF ORIGAMI

The beginnings of origami are shrouded in mystery. Paper was invented in China sometime around 206 BC and was introduced to Japan in the early seventh century. The Japanese refined the manufacturing process to make paper both softer and more durable. We can assume that origami emerged soon after, given the human tendency to create and explore new uses for things.

The word *origami* comes from the Japanese *ori*, meaning 'to fold' and *kami*, meaning 'paper'. As the name suggests, the goal is to transform a single piece of flat (generally square) paper into a model using only folding and sculpting. Historically, cutting and gluing were discouraged, although some designs include judicious use of these additional techniques.

Folded paper was originally used only in religious ceremonies, due to its high cost. But over time, origami started to be practised more widely, with symbolic paper decorations, such as butterflies, commonly used for weddings.

Origami ultimately became a popular recreational pursuit, enjoyed by people of varying ages and from different walks of life. Origami made its way into European cultures sometime in the fifteenth century. It may have been imported by the Moors, who themselves may have encountered it in Japan or China (where it is called *Zhe Zhi*).

Origami's popularity over time is probably due to two main reasons. First, paper folding can be extremely relaxing. It perfectly marries simplicity and complexity and requires a great deal of concentration to do properly, especially with more complex folds and activities. Second, at the end you are rewarded with interesting, beautiful models that can be used as decorations — or even given as gifts, as we will explore in this book. ■

MINDFUL ORIGAMI

Origami is a great way to develop mindfulness. Mindfulness refers to the ability to be fully present and engaged in each moment. It involves focusing on what is actually happening in the senses — that is, what we can see, hear, feel, taste or smell — rather than being caught up in distraction or thinking. With practice, we can learn to recognize when the attention has wandered somewhere else, and simply redirect it back to the senses once again.

As we do this repeatedly, we get much better at keeping the attention in the present, and at noticing when it has wandered. We also get better at bringing it straight back, without thinking about or evaluating what we were distracted by — or giving ourselves a hard time for getting distracted in the first place. We can also cultivate qualities like curiosity, gentleness and self-compassion through mindfulness practice. In fact, anything we practise, we get better at!

Research is increasingly showing that cultivating mindfulness produces a range of benefits including better mental and physical health, and improved study/work performance. It even rewires key parts of the brain such as the prefrontal cortex and hippocampus, both of which are involved in learning and healthy functioning. So we can literally rewire our brain for happiness through practising mindfulness.

Mindfulness is commonly cultivated through meditation, which really just means 'attention training'. It can also be developed through informal practices, simply meaning that we bring our full attention to whatever we are doing in each moment, whether this be eating, cleaning our teeth, communicating, working or travelling.

Obviously, origami is an excellent way to practise mindfulness. Setting time aside to engage fully with the simple act of paper folding means that we start to cultivate presence, focus, curiosity and patience. We can enjoy the texture of the paper, the feeling of making delicate creases and the visual feast of the different colours and shapes. ▓

HOW TO USE THIS BOOK

The Art of Mindful Origami includes fifteen different activities, starting with simple designs and increasing in complexity as you master basic techniques. These are:

I have provided beautiful paper for you to tear out and use. Some of the sheets can be coloured in, so you can customize your models. You may wish to get additional paper and make multiple versions of different sizes and colours. With some of the more complex models, you may also wish to practise on plain paper before attempting them using the included coloured paper.

Where possible, I give some background on where each of the models has come from. Some of them have very interesting uses and powerful stories associated with them.

Just folding the models is an excellent mindfulness practice in itself. However, for those wanting to take their mindfulness to the next level, I have also included additional exercises that you can do with each of the models. These involve engaging more fully with the world around you and cultivating qualities of mindfulness such as curiosity and generosity. ▓

BASIC FOLDING TECHNIQUES

Throughout *The Art of Mindful Origami* a number of symbols are used to represent different techniques. There are also some basic folding techniques that are used in most models, as in the following illustration.

   As you work your way through this book, you should also keep in mind the following:

1. Follow the instructions carefully. Skipping steps or making folds incorrectly will confuse you, may make the model look funny and could make subsequent steps harder. If you get lost, just unfold the last thing you did and go back a step. Remember to breathe. Fold each crease neatly and fully. You should run your thumbnail (or a flat edge such as a ruler) along it — unless the instructions say not to, as is the case for some folds.

2. Be patient. We tend to seek instant results, and this can show up when we are doing origami. Being focused on the outcome will get in the way of enjoying the process (and doing it well). This is true of anything in life. The whole point of this book is to help you slow down and be in the moment, so practise this when you are folding the models.

3. On a related note, if you get frustrated or tense, just take a short break. Perhaps note where you are up to, put the model down and simply breathe and release physical tension from your body. Can you notice what is happening in your mind that is creating the tension or frustration? This is a great skill to cultivate in day-to-day life, too.

Have fun! ▨

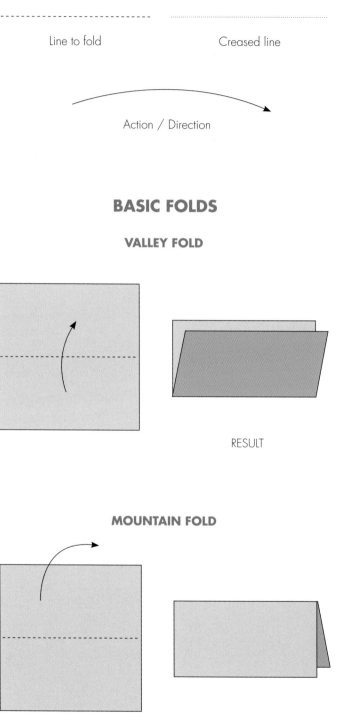

SYMBOLS

Line to fold   Creased line

Action / Direction

BASIC FOLDS

VALLEY FOLD

RESULT

MOUNTAIN FOLD

RESULT

UNFOLD

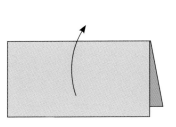

RESULT (Dotted line shows crease)

FOLD & UNFOLD

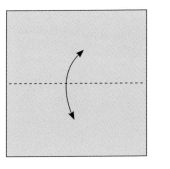

RESULT

PLEAT

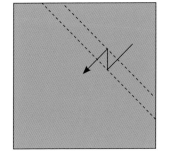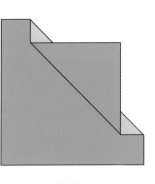

RESULT

ROTATE

RESULT

TURN OVER

RESULT

PUSH CORNER INSIDE

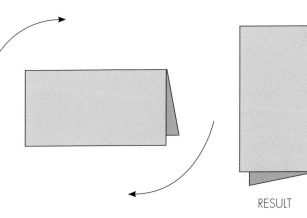

RESULT

GIFT BOX

The origami box is a simple activity, and you end up with a handy box. You can even make a second box and use it as a lid.

You can then store things in it (like your secret stash of sweets). Even better, you can use it as wrapping for gifts.

If you want to make a lid (or even a number of boxes), make multiple copies of the design on the next page. Enlarge or shrink the copies to make boxes of different sizes.

HOW TO FOLD

STEP 1

Start with printed side down. Mountain fold in half vertically and horizontally, unfolding each time. Remember that a mountain fold means the crease points up toward you.

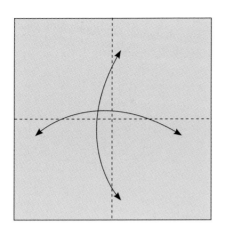

STEP 2

Fold the four corners in toward the centre point.

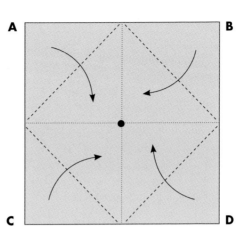

STEP 3

Now fold each edge to the centre point, one at a time, unfolding each before folding the next.

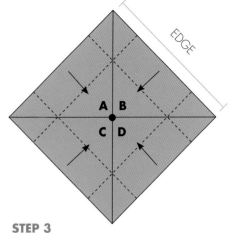

STEP 4

Unfold two of the corners, as shown.

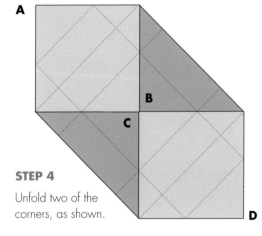

STEP 5

Re-crease the valley folds, as shown, and unfold.

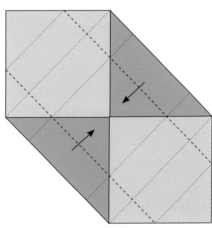

STEP 6

Fold in E and F to the point shown, raising the side up at the same time. Make sure the side folds along the crease, as shown.

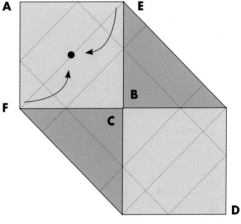

STEP 7

Fold down the side along the crease, as shown.

STEP 8

Repeat on the other side.

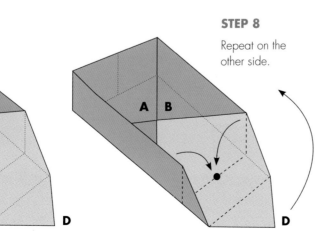

COMPLETED

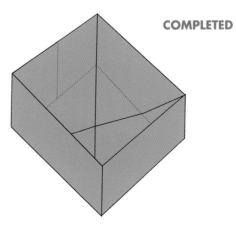

THE GIFT OF MINDFUL GIVING

In this exercise, you can give your box to someone as a gift. We all know how amazing it feels to receive gifts. And it feels even better to give them. Studies have shown that generosity and giving reduce stress, boost our happiness and even extend how long we live.

1. Take a few moments to close your eyes and focus on your breathing. Once you have become present, have a think about the people in your life who you care about the most.

2. Choose one of these people and bring them to mind. Really picture them in front of you, seeing their face. Tune in to the sense of connection and notice how this feels in your body, particularly in your heart. If you have mixed feelings, just tune in to the sense of warmth, connectedness and love. Take a few moments to really enjoy these sensations.

3. Think about the things this person likes. What are their favourite sweets? What other small gifts would they appreciate?

4. Get these things and put them in the box, along with a small note expressing your gratitude for this person being in your life.

You might like to write the note on a folded heart (see p. 35). You could even fold a number of hearts and simply fill the box with little messages of appreciation.

5. Next time you see the person, give them the gift. Watch their face as they open it and read the note (or eat the sweets). You might like to help them with this last part — mindfully of course!

As a variation, you can make a series of boxes, each slightly smaller than the last (just use incrementally smaller squares of paper). Then you can decorate each and put them one inside each other to make nested boxes. Then when the person opens it, it will be like a pass-the-parcel (remember that from when you were a kid?)

You might also like to give a gift to someone who needs some cheering up. Here, along with the sweets, you might like to write down a number of things you like about them and give them a box of gratitude.

Encourage them to pay it forward so that they too can experience the benefits of generosity. ■

DRINKING CUP

This classical origami pattern is fun to make and extremely useful too. If you rub wax onto the paper (or use pre-waxed paper) you can actually drink out of it. Made with regular paper, it can be used to hold paperclips or other small items.

HOW TO FOLD

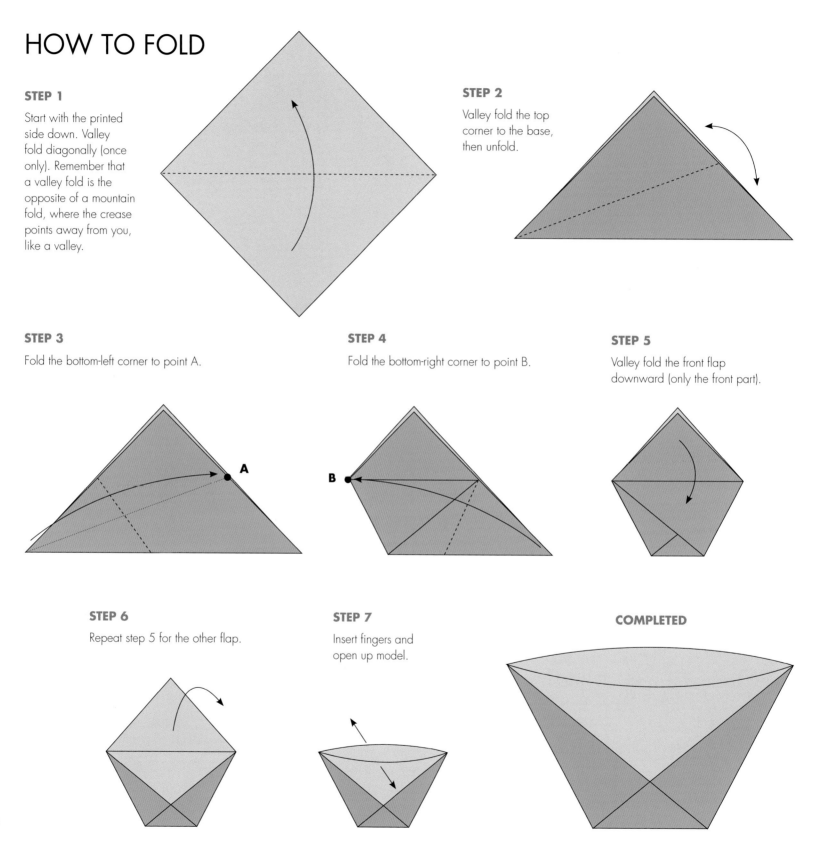

STEP 1

Start with the printed side down. Valley fold diagonally (once only). Remember that a valley fold is the opposite of a mountain fold, where the crease points away from you, like a valley.

STEP 2

Valley fold the top corner to the base, then unfold.

STEP 3

Fold the bottom-left corner to point A.

A

STEP 4

Fold the bottom-right corner to point B.

B

STEP 5

Valley fold the front flap downward (only the front part).

STEP 6

Repeat step 5 for the other flap.

STEP 7

Insert fingers and open up model.

COMPLETED

MINDFUL DRINKING

There is an old story about some monks who set out to demonstrate the power of mindfulness to the king, who was sceptical that people could develop such a quality through training. The monks each carried bowls filled to the brim with oil through the palace. They were followed by the king's guards, who had orders to strike them down with swords if a single drop were spilled. Despite the obvious stress of this situation (and you thought *you* had a stressful job!), no oil was spilled and the king embraced mindfulness for himself and his subjects.

While most of us would probably rather avoid such extreme ways of cultivating mindfulness, we can use simple activities throughout the day to do so. Many people now practise mindful eating, which has been shown to be very beneficial for physical and mental health (and means that people end up practising mindfulness at least three times a day). Mindful eating simply requires slowing down, removing distractions and fully engaging with the sensory experience of eating.

We can do the same thing with drinking, whether this be our tea or coffee in the morning, our wine at night, or just glasses of water throughout the day. Slowing down just a little and intentionally connecting with each aspect of the experience is all it takes.

For this exercise, you might like to take a candle and wax the inside of your drinking cup origami model. It might be easier to do this before you have folded it (if you do this, wax the plain side of the paper, corner to corner). Or you might like to use a regular glass or cup for the exercise instead.

Pour some water or other liquid into the cup, paying close attention and ensuring that you don't spill a single drop. Feel the sensation of the cup in your hands as you lift it to your lips. Take a sip, and feel the liquid on your lips and in your mouth. Taste it fully. Feel it as it goes down your throat. Savour the experience.

Next time you make some tea, tune in to each part of the process: filling and boiling the kettle, placing the leaves or teabag into the pot or cup, pouring the water, waiting, stirring or jiggling. Notice the taste of the tea and the sensation of drinking it. Savour the enjoyment.

You may like to do the same with *everything* you drink throughout the day. ▪

SAIL BOAT

Boats represent freedom. Wouldn't you just love to be able to pull up anchor and sail somewhere new whenever you wanted? They also represent buoyancy — the ability to stay afloat and ride out any storm.

If you would like to expand this activity, you could make a few boats out of different coloured paper, and then string them together to form a wonderful mobile. You could perhaps use pieces of driftwood from the beach and even include some shells as added decoration.

HOW TO FOLD

STEP 1

Start with the paper right side up. Valley fold in half diagonally, then unfold and valley fold in half again. Unfold. Turn paper over.

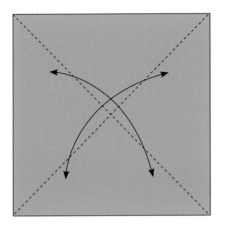

STEP 2

Valley fold in half to create a crease across the centre, then fold in half again. Unfold.

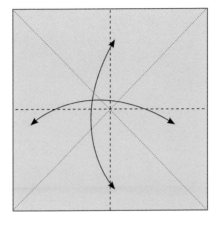

STEP 3

Fold corner A towards the centre point, then similarly fold corners B and C towards the centre, as shown.

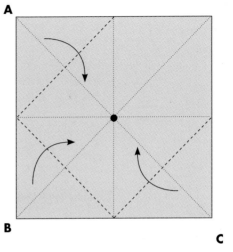

STEP 4

Fold point A down and crease along the line, as shown.

STEP 5

Pinch the centre line in, bringing point A and point B up to form the sails. Flatten the model.

STEP 6

Fold the bottom of the model under, as shown.

COMPLETED

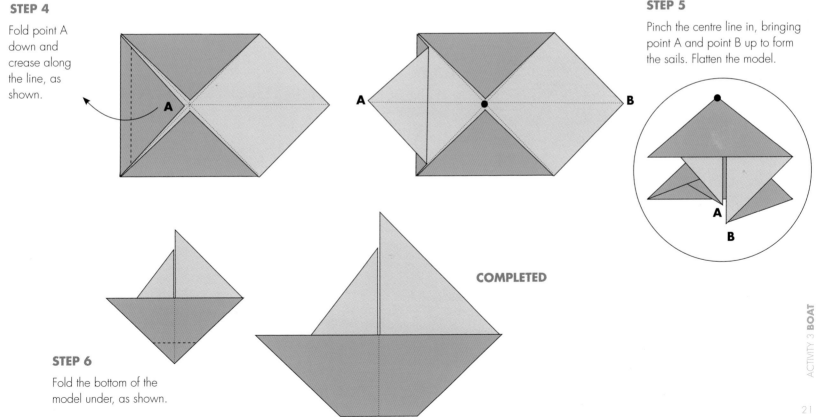

RIDING THE WAVES OF YOUR BREATH

Breath is life. From the moment we are born to the moment we die, we are breathing. The word 'inspiration' literally means to breathe life into something.

Because it is always happening, the breath is also an excellent anchor for mindfulness. Anytime we tune in and feel the breath as it is, without thinking about it or trying to control it, we bring our attention into the present.

Our breath also changes when we are stressed and anxious. So if we remain aware of our breath throughout the day, we can notice when it becomes higher in our chest or changes in some way — giving us an excellent window into our own internal emotional state. We can literally use the breath as a barometer for our own internal weather.

In this exercise, you can use the boat you have made to cultivate awareness of your breathing.

Lie down somewhere comfortable. Balance your boat on your belly. Notice how it rocks up and down as you breathe, as if it were riding waves on the ocean.

Trust that your body knows how to breathe perfectly well without you trying to control it. It does a perfectly good job of this each night as you sleep! Simply notice the natural expansion and contraction of your belly — the rising and falling — by watching how your boat pitches up and down.

If your mind wanders off (and it will — this is normal, remember), just bring it back as soon as you notice. See what happens when you bring it back gently, without judging or criticising yourself.

As you focus on your boat rocking on the waves of your breath, what do you notice? Does your breath change? Does it find its own natural rhythm? Does it get deeper or shallower?

Remember, the object of this exercise is to simply observe the breath *as it is*, rather than trying to change it.

After you have rocked the boat on the waves of your breath for 5 to 10 minutes, can you remain aware of your breath throughout the day? Can you notice when it changes (and learn to catch the storms in your mind)? ■

CRANE

The paper crane is probably the most famous of all origami models. In Japan, China and Korea, the crane is a sacred creature and believed to live for a thousand years.

Cranes represent longevity, happiness and fortune. They were believed to carry the souls of the dead to paradise.

HOW TO FOLD

STEP 1

Start with the printed side down. Valley fold diagonally both ways, unfolding each time.

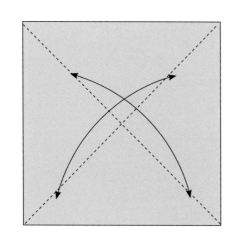

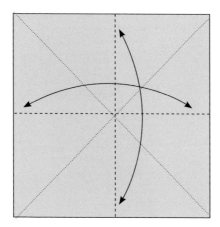

STEP 2

Valley fold horizontally and vertically, unfolding each time.

STEP 3

Fold corners A, B and C to meet bottom corner D. Start with corner A, then B and lastly C.

STEP 4

Fold the left and right sides of the top layer only towards the centre line.

STEP 5

Fold the top behind.

STEP 6

Open the sides back out and then lift the upper layer. The sides will fold in to look like a beak. Flatten.

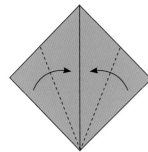

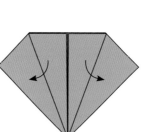

STEP 7

Turn model over.

STEP 8

Repeat step 4.

STEP 9

Repeat step 6.

STEP 10

Fold the front flap on the left and right inward nearly to the centre. A small gap will make it easier for your reverse folds in the next step.

STEP 11

Turn model over.

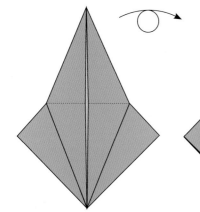

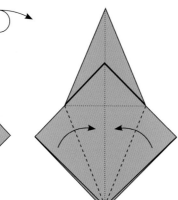

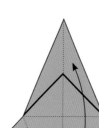

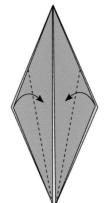

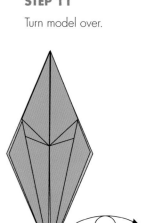

STEP 12

Repeat step 10.

STEP 13

Fold the bottom points upwards and to the sides. Then fold one of the points to make a head (see close-up).

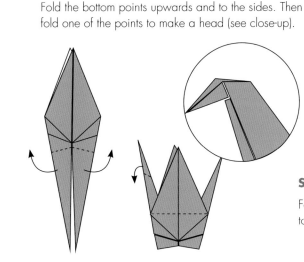

STEP 14

Fold both sides down to create wings.

COMPLETED

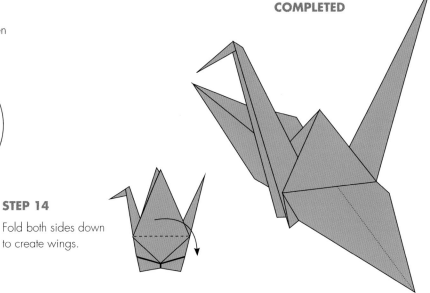

A THOUSAND PAPER CRANES

The story of Sadako Sasaki is very well known, even outside Japan. As an infant, Sadako survived the atomic bombing of Hiroshima. Sadly, at age twelve she was diagnosed with leukaemia, as were many survivors of the attacks.

There is a Japanese tradition that anyone who folds one thousand paper cranes (called *senbazuru*, and commonly strung together on 25 strings of 40 cranes each) will be granted one wish. So Sadako set out to fold them, intending to wish for healing. However, she only managed to fold 644 cranes before she died. Her classmates folded the remaining number and she was buried with them.

Cranes came to symbolize the wish for peace, hope and healing. Every year thousands of strings of *senbazuru* are draped over a statue of Sadako — a little girl holding a paper crane in her hand — in the Hiroshima Peace Park.

The legend says that to have your wish granted, you must make all the cranes yourself and keep them. However, strings of cranes have also become popular gifts.

You might like to make a full *senbazuru* and then make a wish, perhaps for your own healing or that of someone else. You have to make them all yourself, and some traditions hold that you have to make them within a single year.

Alternatively, you could make a string of cranes (or even just fold a single crane) and give it to someone special to you. Perhaps there is someone in your life in need of some healing? Keep this person in your heart as you fold the crane/s and pay attention to the look on their face and the feeling in your body when you give it to them.

Research shows that when we cultivate attitudes like love and compassion, we release neurotransmitters such as dopamine and serotonin, and the hormone oxytocin. These are very beneficial for our health and wellbeing. One of the secrets to life is that our happiness lies in the happiness of others. ■

STAR

Stars represent wishes and wonder. Can you remember all the songs from your childhood about wishing on stars and wondering what they were?

Stars also represent achievement and completion. They are placed on top of Christmas trees, and students are sometimes given star-shaped stickers to recognize them doing well.

The origami star can be used as decoration or given as a gift.

HOW TO FOLD

STEP 1

Start with the printed side down. Mountain fold vertically and horizontally, unfolding each time. Turn page over once unfolded.

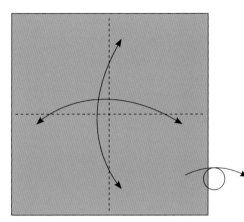

STEP 2

Valley fold diagonally (both ways), unfolding each time.

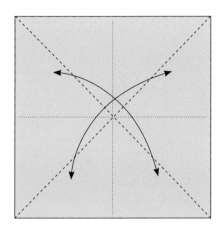

STEP 3

Bring point A to point B. Then tuck in the bottom two corners to meet point B, to make a triangle.

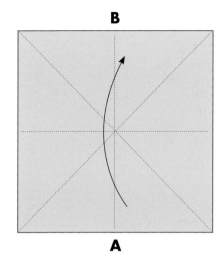

STEP 4

Fold both sides in along the creases shown. Repeat on the other side.

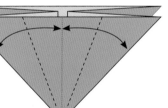

STEP 5

Pleat both sides along the new crease shown. The easiest way to do this is to fold edge A to the existing valley fold B and then fold the flap back along its original valley fold (which becomes a mountain fold). If you get confused, just unfold again, take a few mindful breaths, look closely at the diagram and try again. Flip model over and repeat. This time should be much easier as you can use the other side as a guide for where the fold needs to be.

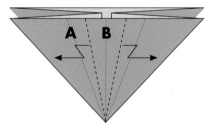

STEP 6

Fold the top two points at the same time along the dotted line shown. Fold and spread them so that they form the two remaining points of the star. You may need to turn the model over a bit to see. As you flatten them down, you will see the centre part of the model opens out in a square pattern. Flatten the two triangles A and B. This will make the whole model flat.

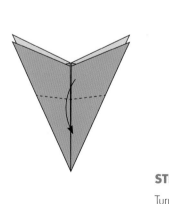

STEP 7

Turn model over.

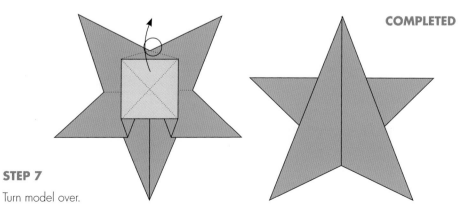

COMPLETED

TWINKLE, TWINKLE, LITTLE STAR

After folding the star model, take it outside at night. Look up into the sky and gaze at the other stars in the sky above. If you live in the city you might only see a few of the really bright ones — probably the planets Mercury, Venus, Mars, Jupiter and Saturn. If you are in the countryside you may be treated to a three-dimensional vista of thousands of stars. (Hint: go out into nature more often!)

Even though mindfulness begins with bringing our full attention to what is happening in the five senses, we can also bring mindfulness to our thoughts. So, as you gaze at the stars, you might like to do a mindful reflection.

Consider for a moment that the Earth you are standing (or lying) on is a tiny planet orbiting a mid-sized sun at the edge of the Milky Way. The other stars you see are planets from our solar system, the suns of other solar systems, and in many cases are themselves entire galaxies.

Feel the contact your body makes with the ground and notice the effects of gravity. Tune in to the way the ground supports you, holding you up. Get a sense of the Earth underneath you, supporting you.

If your attention wanders anywhere other than this reflection or direct sensory experience, simply bring it back again. This noticing and coming back is the foundation of mindfulness practice.

Take some mindful breaths. Appreciate how the air contains just the right mix of gases to sustain life. Reflect on how the vast blackness you are gazing at doesn't have any of these gases. Take a moment to be grateful for your breath.

Notice if a sense of gratitude for the Earth and its life-sustaining properties appears. What does this feel like in your body? How does it affect your thinking and actions? ■

PINWHEEL

Remember those pinwheels you used to get at fairs as a kid? Well, now you can make one! They make great decorations and even toys on windy days or when you are travelling in a car.

As well as the paper from the book, you will also need to get a pencil, a straw or stick and a small pin for this model.

HOW TO FOLD

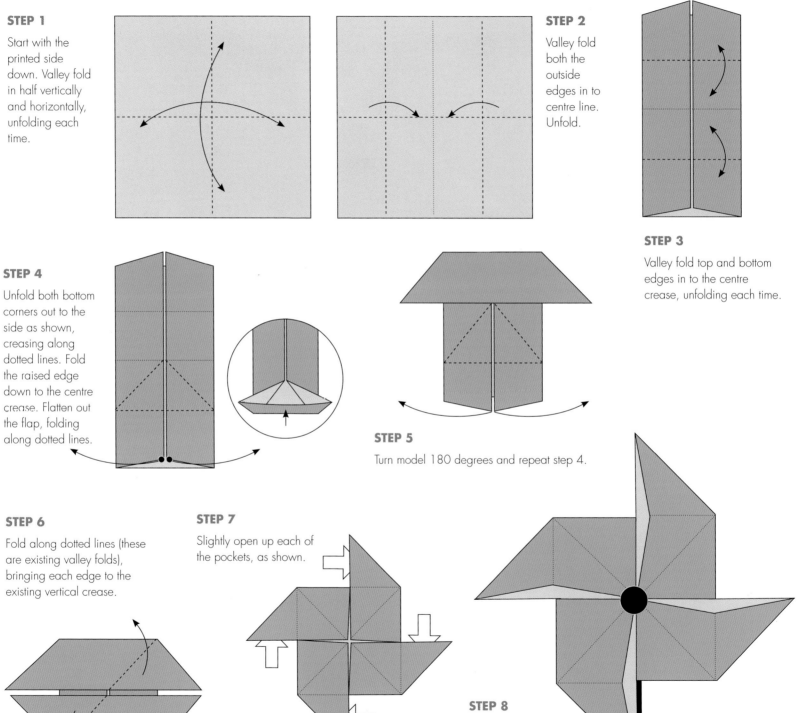

STEP 1

Start with the printed side down. Valley fold in half vertically and horizontally, unfolding each time.

STEP 2

Valley fold both the outside edges in to centre line. Unfold.

STEP 3

Valley fold top and bottom edges in to the centre crease, unfolding each time.

STEP 4

Unfold both bottom corners out to the side as shown, creasing along dotted lines. Fold the raised edge down to the centre crease. Flatten out the flap, folding along dotted lines.

STEP 5

Turn model 180 degrees and repeat step 4.

STEP 6

Fold along dotted lines (these are existing valley folds), bringing each edge to the existing vertical crease.

STEP 7

Slightly open up each of the pockets, as shown.

STEP 8

Pin the model to a straw or stick.

COMPLETED

MINDFULNESS MEDITATION

If you have already made some of the models in the book, you will have had more than enough opportunity to practise mindfulness. Perhaps you have noticed how, when you are really focused on getting a crisp fold done, your attention is engaged fully in the moment. And how when you are engaged and present, you are no longer caught up in worries and concerns.

You don't have to push these things away — they just go. That's because in each moment we are *either* caught up in the default mode of daydreaming and mind-wandering (which usually means worrying, dwelling or reacting) or we are engaged and present. This is the basic principle of mindfulness, and is why it is so good for both our wellbeing and performance.

While we can cultivate mindfulness through activities like origami, we can also develop it through meditation. The word 'meditation' really means 'attention training' and mindfulness meditation simply involves training our attention to be in the present. We do this by focusing on what is happening in the senses. When we do this repeatedly, we rewire the brain for greater focus and awareness, as well as enhanced wellbeing and study/work performance.

We can use any of the five senses (what we can feel, see, hear, smell or taste) as the object of meditation. Here, we will use the sense of touch, as it is one of the most obvious and easiest to pay attention to. In particular, we will focus on the movement of the breath. Breath is one of the fundamental aspects of being alive, although we tend to take it for granted. It is also an excellent anchor for keeping us present, as well as a way of keeping track of our internal state.

1. Sit comfortably. You can lie down, but you need to ensure that you stay awake during the meditation. This is an exercise in falling awake and zoning in rather than getting sleepy and zoned out. Don't worry too much about your posture, but ensure that your spine is straight yet without tension. Find a posture that embodies alertness and relaxation at the same time.

2. Set a timer for 5 minutes. This is a good amount to start with and you can gradually extend it once you get the hang of meditating.

3. Take a moment to tune in to your body. Take note of the state it is in. Is it tired or energized? Is it tense or relaxed? If you notice tension, see if you can feel the specific muscles that are holding it, and let it go. You can't force the body to relax but you can let go of tension once you notice it.

4. Likewise, notice the state the mind is in. Is it busy with thoughts, or quiet? Is it alert or sleepy and dull? If you get caught up in thinking, let it go and bring your attention back to the body again.

5. Notice the obvious sensations in the body, such as the points of contact with the floor. Feel the pressure, and tune in to the sense of support and stability.

6. Now hold the pinwheel in front of you and blow. Notice it spin as your breath moves through it. Breathe deeply through your nose and blow again. Do this a few times, noticing which parts of your body expand and contract as you breathe in and out.

7. Now put the pinwheel down and allow your breath to return to a natural rhythm. Don't try to change it, for example by trying to breathe deeply. Trust that your body knows perfectly well how to breathe (it does a great job of it while you are asleep at night) and that it will find its own depth and rhythm if you let it. Allow the body to breathe naturally and simply feel the expansion and contraction, the rising and falling of the breath. Perhaps you can even feel the air as it enters and leaves the nostrils, or in the back of your throat.

8. Find where in your body the breathing is most obvious and rest your attention there. Simply notice what it feels like to breathe in and out. Is the breath deep or shallow? Is its texture rough and course or smooth and silky? What else do you notice about the breath when you pay attention to it in this way?

9. Can you notice the points where the breath turns around? At the top of the in-breath and the bottom of the out-breath, it definitely turns — although if you pay enough attention you will notice that there is no actual pause.

10. When your attention wanders off (which it inevitably will, by the way) simply notice where it has gone and return it to the breath once again. See if you can do this without getting annoyed or judgmental that your mind has wandered, or thinking about whatever has distracted you.

11. Continue to breathe in this way until the alarm or timer goes off. Take a moment to check back in with your body and mind, noticing any differences compared to the start of the meditation.

Research shows that people who practise mindfulness meditation on a daily basis, even just for 5 to 10 minutes at a time, experience a range of benefits for their physical and mental health.

Doing it first thing every morning, before you get caught up in the routine of your day, is generally the best time, although for some people mid-morning or evenings can be better. Put the pinwheel somewhere to remind you to practise.

It is also very useful to be aware of the breath throughout the day. This keeps us grounded and present. And because the breath changes when we are stressed or upset, paying attention to it throughout the day gives us a very good window into our internal states — and early warning when we start to get upset.

You might want to use this strategy when attempting some of the more challenging models later in this book! ■

SAMURAI HELMET

In ancient Japan, samurai warriors were known to attach *noshi* to gifts they gave to other samurai. *Noshi* are white paper folded with a strip of dried abalone or other meat, and are considered a token of good fortune.

One of the first origami patterns made by many children is the samurai helmet. It is a fun piece to make and is visually impressive when it is done. It is also possible to fold it out of newspaper to make a full-sized, wearable version.

HOW TO FOLD

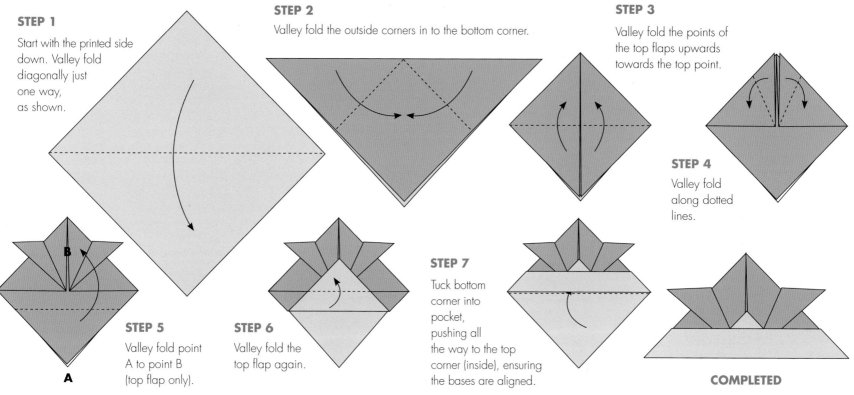

STEP 1

Start with the printed side down. Valley fold diagonally just one way, as shown.

STEP 2

Valley fold the outside corners in to the bottom corner.

STEP 3

Valley fold the points of the top flaps upwards towards the top point.

STEP 4

Valley fold along dotted lines.

STEP 5

Valley fold point A to point B (top flap only).

STEP 6

Valley fold the top flap again.

STEP 7

Tuck bottom corner into pocket, pushing all the way to the top corner (inside), ensuring the bases are aligned.

COMPLETED

A DAY IN THE LIFE OF A SAMURAI

Samurai were renowned for living their lives according to a strict warrior code, called *Bushido*. Literally meaning 'way of the warrior', this code emphasized loyalty, honour and simplicity. The fundamental underpinnings of this way of life rested on wisdom and serenity, and were a necessary counterpoint to the often brutal lifestyle of a professional soldier.

Bushido includes eight virtues. These are: self-control, courage, righteousness, benevolence, respect, sincerity, honour and loyalty.

While most of us luckily don't need to carry swords any more, we would do well to cultivate some of these values and virtues in our lives. The busyness and distraction of modern life often means that we become reactive and stressed, and may not operate at our best.

For the rest of today, slow down a little and be more present. Practise mindful presence during each activity and each moment.

How does doing this influence the things that you do and say?

As an additional experiment, see if you can go a whole day without telling a lie. Even when they consider themselves to be generally quite honest, many people who do this experiment discover that they have a tendency to fudge the truth at times, or omit certain information. What happens when you stop doing this? How do you feel inside? What happens in your mind? Your relationships? Of course, it's necessary to combine this with an attitude of non-harming, which is an important aspect of mindfulness. Don't go around being brutally honest, hurting people's feelings in the process. Instead, seek to find a balance between being truthful and being kind. According to many wisdom traditions, the deepest kind of honesty arises naturally from perceiving directly the interconnectedness between all things. Use mindfulness to help you explore this. ■

HEART

The heart is one of the physical foundations of life, and is a symbol of love and connectedness.

This origami heart can be attached to the front of an envelope or card and given to someone you love. It also forms a wonderful decoration for weddings and other special events. You might even like to fold a number of them, write little messages of appreciation on them, and fill an origami box (see p. 14) with them as a gift for someone special.

HOW TO FOLD

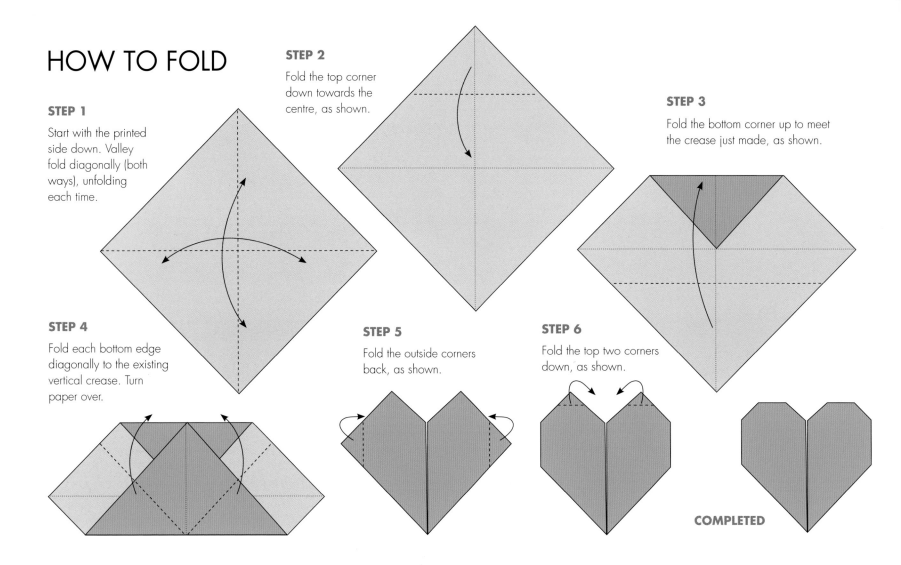

STEP 1

Start with the printed side down. Valley fold diagonally (both ways), unfolding each time.

STEP 2

Fold the top corner down towards the centre, as shown.

STEP 3

Fold the bottom corner up to meet the crease just made, as shown.

STEP 4

Fold each bottom edge diagonally to the existing vertical crease. Turn paper over.

STEP 5

Fold the outside corners back, as shown.

STEP 6

Fold the top two corners down, as shown.

COMPLETED

CULTIVATING HEARTFULNESS

The neuroscience of mindfulness tells us that anything we practise gets hardwired into our brain. We get better at it, and if we practise it regularly it becomes our new default mode of functioning.

Loving-kindness (sometimes called *metta*) meditation is a powerful way of cultivating heartfulness. It might be better described as 'sending kind thoughts' as it involves cultivating attitudes of unconditional friendliness and goodwill and sending kind wishes to others and ourselves. Research shows that when we do this,

we enhance our own mental and physical wellbeing and our relationships become more harmonious.

While loving-kindness meditation differs from classical mindfulness meditation exercises (such as the one we explored earlier on p. 31), it is in fact a central attitude of mindfulness and one that we cultivate any time we are practising mindfulness correctly.

1. Sit or lie comfortably. Ground yourself by tuning in to the sensations in your body, especially the points of contact with the chair or ground and the movement of your breath.

2. Bring to mind someone you love and have a good connection with. If multiple people come to mind, just pick one. It could even be a pet or spiritual figure if you like. Imagine them in front of you at a comfortable distance. See their face. Tune in to the connection between you and notice how this feels in your body, especially in your heart.

3. After a couple of minutes, stay with this sense of goodwill in your heart but let go of the image of this person. Instead, bring your attention more to yourself. Cultivate a felt sense of goodwill for yourself and make the following wishes:

- 'May I be happy'
- 'May I be healthy'
- 'May I be peaceful and content'
- 'May I be safe from harm'.

Repeat these wishes to yourself at a comfortable pace, as many times as you like (for at least a couple of minutes). You may like to wish additional, specific things for yourself, or just go with the basic wish, 'May I be happy'. Focus on the sensations in your heart, although if you can't feel anything, just focus on the wishes.

4. Now bring to mind someone you love. It might be the same person as before, or it might be someone new. Again, just pick one person and stick with them. Allow the feeling of goodwill to radiate out to them (you might even visualize light or warmth flowing out to them) and send kind wishes their way: 'May you be happy', 'May you be well' etc.

If your mind wanders during this (it will!) simply return your attention to the image of the person, the wishes, or even to your breath or body sensations.

5. After a few minutes, let go of the image of this person and bring to mind someone you are aware of, but don't have particularly strong positive or negative feelings toward. Actually, this is most people in our lives — our neighbours, colleagues, bus drivers, someone we passed in the street earlier. Send kind wishes their way: 'May you be happy', 'May you be well' etc.

6. Now bring to mind someone you have difficulty with. Don't go for your worst enemy here, someone who is immediately going to close your heart. Just pick someone you have some conflict with or something unresolved. Again, see them in front of you. See their face. Notice any tensing or closing in your body. Can you feel the suffering in it for you? Can you release this tension a little?

Reflect on the fact that happy people are easy to be around, and difficult people tend to be unhappy. That's why they are difficult! So from a logical standpoint it actually makes sense to wish happiness for them, as strange as this might seem.

7. Send kind wishes their way: 'May you be happy', 'May you be well' etc. Even if this feels mechanical or if you are just saying the words, keep sending the wishes out. Very often, people are surprised how this can transform difficult relationships. At the very least, you will stop tensing yourself up by holding onto resentment.

8. Finally, broaden your awareness to include yourself once again, as well as all of your loved ones, all the strangers and all the people you have difficulty with. See if you can hold all of these people in your awareness at once — hold them all in your heart. You might like to include everyone on Earth, as well as animals and other beings. You might even like to let this awareness expand out to embrace the whole universe and any conscious beings that might be out there.

Allow the felt sense of goodwill to radiate out from your heart in all directions. Sense your interconnectedness with all beings and send kind wishes out to them all: 'May all beings be happy', 'May all beings be well' etc.

9. As you finish up, take a few moments to tune in to your own body and mind once again. Notice the effects of the meditation. Can you feel a sense of relaxation, warmth and wellbeing? That's the effect of oxytocin, sometimes referred to as the 'love hormone', being released.

Doing this meditation regularly will hardwire qualities of heartfulness into your brain. It is also an excellent way to reduce conflict with others, or to short-circuit self-criticism. ▪

FOX

In Asian folklore foxes were seen as magical beings, able to shape-shift into human form. They could be faithful guardians and friends, and at times could be tricksters.

Whether naughty or nice, one thing foxes definitely are, is cute. Especially origami foxes! This model can be used to adorn cards or presents and is bound to bring a smile to whoever it is given to.

HOW TO FOLD

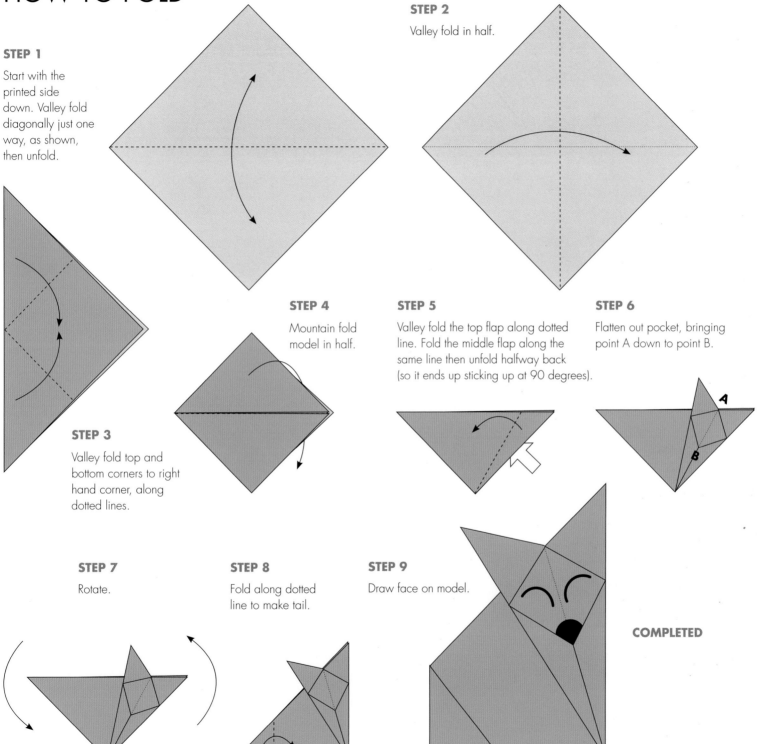

STEP 1

Start with the printed side down. Valley fold diagonally just one way, as shown, then unfold.

STEP 2

Valley fold in half.

STEP 3

Valley fold top and bottom corners to right hand corner, along dotted lines.

STEP 4

Mountain fold model in half.

STEP 5

Valley fold the top flap along dotted line. Fold the middle flap along the same line then unfold halfway back (so it ends up sticking up at 90 degrees).

STEP 6

Flatten out pocket, bringing point A down to point B.

STEP 7

Rotate.

STEP 8

Fold along dotted line to make tail.

STEP 9

Draw face on model.

COMPLETED

MOVE LIKE A FOX

Foxes have a great sense of body awareness and excellent balance, which lets them move very fluidly. They are also very sneaky and are justifiably wary of humans. We can therefore learn a lot from them about moving efficiently.

Mindful movement is a wonderful way of bringing mindfulness more fully into our day. It simply involves bringing awareness to how we are moving — to things like the activation of our muscles, the shifting balance, the points of contact, what we notice around us as we travel.

Mindfulness doesn't have to be done slowly — it just has to be done mindfully! — but slowing down a little can be good in the beginning. This allows us to tune in more fully to the experience of moving. When we have developed this base level of awareness, we can go back to doing things at full speed again.

Here are some hints for weaving mindful movement into your day:

1. When you wake up in the morning, take a moment to check in with your body. Have a stretch, in a natural way like you did when you were little. Take a few mindful breaths.

2. Then get out of bed, noticing which foot hits the floor first. What does it feel like to go from lying to standing?

3. Take a mindful shower. Many people stand under the water planning their day or daydreaming, completely missing the wonderfully relaxing experience of warm water on their skin. Tune in to this and take a moment to appreciate how lucky you are to even have hot showers.

4. Take a few minutes to sit and meditate. Set a timer for 5 minutes and simply sit and follow your breathing, perhaps following the instructions on page 30 for mindfulness meditation. It is that easy.

5. As you leave the house, pause at the door and check your intention for the day. What do you want to get done today? If you can't think of an intention, one that I suggest is to see how useful you can be for others. Research shows that altruism and compassion significantly increase our own happiness.

6. Stay present as you travel to work or school (or wherever you are going). Notice how easily your mind rushes off to the destination and starts planning what you will do when you get there. Notice what happens when you keep your attention in your body, noticing your feet hitting the ground, the feeling of the steering wheel in your hand, or the other passengers on the bus.

7. If you are late you can even walk very quickly and yet keep your attention grounded in your body. Notice how this helps you stay calm and relaxed instead of getting flustered.

8. As you work or study, remain aware of your posture. Ensure you are sitting in a way that is good for your body. Take regular opportunities to stand up and stretch and move about. When you walk to the photocopier or kitchen, do it mindfully, enjoying the movement and noticing what you pass on the way. Smile at people.

9. When exercising, whether in the gym or outside, experiment with not having music on or watching the television. Use the time as an opportunity to practise being mindful instead, just by tuning in to your body. Notice what state your body and mind are in. When we pay attention, we are much more aware of what is really happening, and there is the possibility of learning new things. Many athletes are using mindfulness now, not just to calm and focus their minds but to enhance their body awareness, improve their efficiency and minimize injuries. ■

PUPPY FACE

Just in case the fox wasn't cute enough for you — a puppy face! These adorable models can adorn anything from cards to presents. It even warms the heart just to make them and leave them on the fridge or somewhere else you will see them.

Puppies embody playfulness and adventure, and it is good to be reminded about these vital human qualities on a regular basis.

HOW TO FOLD

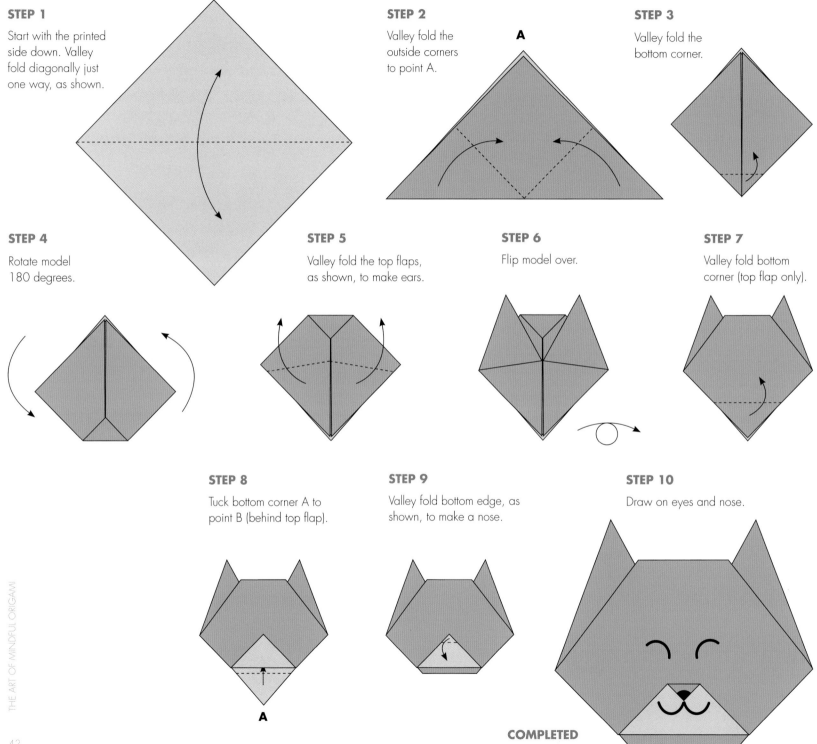

STEP 1

Start with the printed side down. Valley fold diagonally just one way, as shown.

STEP 2

Valley fold the outside corners to point A.

STEP 3

Valley fold the bottom corner.

STEP 4

Rotate model 180 degrees.

STEP 5

Valley fold the top flaps, as shown, to make ears.

STEP 6

Flip model over.

STEP 7

Valley fold bottom corner (top flap only).

STEP 8

Tuck bottom corner A to point B (behind top flap).

STEP 9

Valley fold bottom edge, as shown, to make a nose.

STEP 10

Draw on eyes and nose.

COMPLETED

MINDFULNESS AT PLAY

If we watch puppies, other baby animals and even children, one of the first things we notice is how playful they are. So much learning happens early in life through play. Skills are developed, limits are explored and social orders are established, all through trial and error. Even adolescents could be said to be playing when they push limits and experiment with identity.

Sadly, as many people age they lose touch with this sense of playfulness. Structured education, embarrassment over making mistakes and the pressures of busy modern lives mean that many people stop experimenting and exploring, and instead start doing things in predictable, fixed ways.

The famous 'Water Jar Experiment' from the 1940s is a perfect example of this. In this study, once people had learned to solve a problem (in this case, measuring out the right amount of water using jugs of different volumes) in one way, they kept doing this, even after the formula they had figured out stopped working. This is known as the *Einstellung* effect, and for many people this gets in the way of effective learning.

Luckily, when we practise mindfulness we cultivate an attitude that is sometimes called 'beginner's mind'. This involves setting aside what we *think* we know about something and instead experiencing it as it actually *is*. This increases our creativity and flexibility.

We can do this in countless ways. The simplest might be to do some mindful breathing, allowing the breath to happen naturally rather than trying to breathe deeply or otherwise control it. Notice the tendency to want to manipulate the breath (or at the very least, think about or visualize it). What happens when you just let it happen naturally? What can you learn about the very mundane, everyday experience of breathing when you experience it in this way?

This attitude of openness and playfulness can be brought to every moment. See if you can find ways to practise it. Here are some hints.

1. Get out of bed on the other side. Turn on the shower with a different hand. Dry yourself and get dressed in a different order to normal. What happens when you disrupt your usual routine in this way?

2. Have something completely different for breakfast. Make it up, combining things that you wouldn't normally mix together.

3. Travel to work or school taking a different route. Notice how much easier this makes it to be mindfully aware as you travel. What new things do you notice on the way?

4. Approach your work or study with a beginner's mind. How many different ways could you do it? What happens when you do things in different orders? When you set aside your usual assumptions about how things should be, notice how many more possibilities open up for how things could be.

5. Go on a date with your partner (or even take yourself on one). Do something you have never done before. Go some place new.

6. Notice how alive it makes you feel to approach things in this playful, open way. Is there any reason you wouldn't want more of this in your life? What other ways can you find to be playful and creative in your day-to-day life? Hint: the possibilities are limitless.

Put your folded puppy face model somewhere it will remind you to be playful in this way. And whenever you see actual puppies or children, take a moment to observe the joy with which they interact with the world. Use them as a prompt to connect with your own innate playfulness (we never lose this — we just lose touch with it). Make a commitment to experiencing more of this in your own life. ■

BUTTERFLY

In every culture, butterflies are symbols of change and metamorphosis. Caterpillars hibernate in cocoons and emerge completely different to how they went in — and often much more beautiful.

In Japan, origami butterflies symbolize transformation, love and eternity, and are often placed on sake bottles at weddings, commonly in pairs to represent the bride and groom.

HOW TO FOLD

STEP 1

Start with the printed side down. Valley fold diagonally (both ways), unfolding each time.

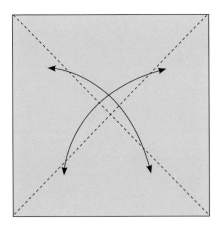

STEP 2

Valley fold both sides to the centre, using the X crease as a guide.

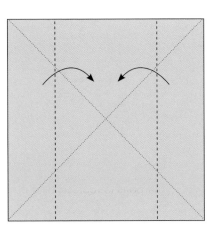

STEP 3

Fold the top and bottom edges to the centre, again using the X as a guide (you will need to peek under the two flaps you just folded).

STEP 4

Insert your fingers inside the pocket you just made (start with the bottom one) and pull out to side. Bring the edge back down to where it was. Flatten model along creases shown. Repeat with top pocket.

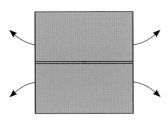

STEP 5

Valley fold the bottom points down, as shown.

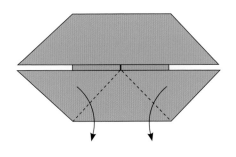

STEP 6

Mountain fold the top towards the back.

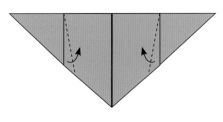

STEP 7

Valley fold the front flaps along the dotted lines, as shown.

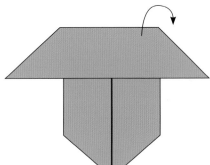

STEP 8

Valley fold model in half along existing central crease.

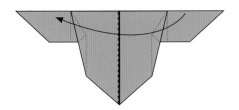

STEP 9

Valley fold top wing, as shown, and unfold.

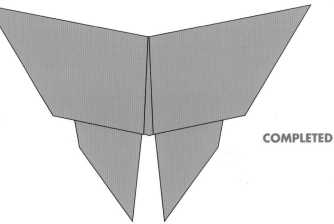

COMPLETED

NOTICING TRANSITIONS

Everything in life is constantly changing. From the tiniest momentary thought flitting through the mind to the seasons, it is a simple fact of reality that everything is always in a state of change and transformation.

However, in our busy, distracted lives we often fail to notice this. Rushing from one activity to the next, often without pausing to even notice we have completed the first, prevents us from noticing this ever-present cycle of change. Living in busy cities tends to divorce us somewhat from our senses and from the cycles of the natural world, further exacerbating the problem.

The good news is that we can reconnect with this reality any time we wish. All we have to do is slow down and pay attention. The following exercise is designed to do exactly this.

1. Stop what you are doing for a moment and tune in to your body. Can you notice your breath? Can you feel how the inhalations expand and fill the body and then at some point this changes into an exhalation as the air leaves again? Follow your breath like this for a few moments.

2. As you tune in to your breath, can you notice how thoughts come and go in the mind? They may be thoughts about breathing or about this exercise, but are just as likely to be entirely random. By staying in touch with the breath, can you notice how thoughts come and go?

3. Look out the window. What time of day is it? Think for a moment about how day becomes night and night becomes day again, as the Earth rotates on its axis. Perhaps you can imagine the Earth rotating in this way — and even imagine it orbiting the sun, with its vertical axis a few degrees off centre, giving rise to the seasons.

4. What season is it where you are right now? If you didn't know this just because of which month it is, what signs are there right in front of you that could let you know? Leaves rustling in piles, snow or grey skies, new shoots on the trees, blazing sunshine? This is the natural cycle of the seasons.

5. If you can see people around you, what age would you estimate they are? Where are they at in their lifespan? Can you see babies who are just starting to toddle or walk? Children who are transitioning to adolescence? Adults towards the end of their lifespan?

6. Where are you at in your own lifespan? What transition are you making? Can you feel your body ageing as you do this very exercise? With each breath you take, with each beat of your heart, you are getting older. Can you sense this directly and accept it, without worrying about it or trying to avoid its reality?

7. What other cycles and transitions can you notice around you right now? Perhaps go for a mindful walk and see what you notice as you explore the world through this framework.

Come back to this simple inquiry as much as you can throughout the day. Step out of all your rushing and start paying attention to the transitions in your day. Even just completing tasks is a form of this. Next time you send that email or tick that thing off the list, pause for a moment and notice that it is done. Tune in to the sense of accomplishment or relief. Really let yourself feel it in your body. Breathe it in. Savour it.

Try to remember to come back to this every time you see a butterfly — both real insects and your own origami model. What effect does it have on your life when you get more in touch with transitions like this? ▧

JUMPING FROG

Action origami models are really fun to make. This simple frog can be made to jump by pressing on its tail and then releasing it.

Schoolchildren have been known to make these and have races. How far can you make yours jump?

HOW TO FOLD

STEP 1

Start with the printed side down. Valley fold vertically.

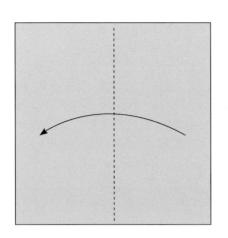

STEP 2

Valley fold top corners to make creases as shown. Unfold.

STEP 3

Valley fold top quarter at the centre of the previous creases. Unfold.

STEP 4

Fold the top down, bringing in the corners as you fold, making the top a point. Use your pre-creased lines.

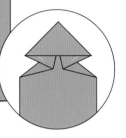

STEP 5

Valley fold the bottom edge to the base of the new triangle.

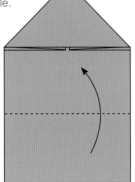

STEP 6

Valley fold the points of the top layer upwards, as shown.

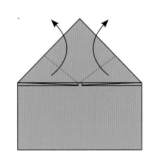

STEP 7

Valley fold the left and right side to meet in the centre.

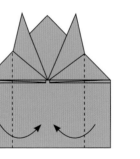

STEP 8

Valley fold along dotted line, then unfold.

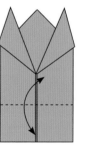

STEP 9

Pull out corners A and B as you fold upwards.

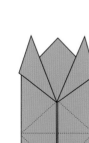

A   **B**

STEP 10

Fold back along dotted lines, as shown.

STEP 11

Fold legs outwards along dotted lines, as shown.

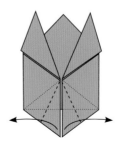

STEP 12

Pleat model along crease, as shown.

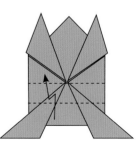

STEP 13

Turn over.

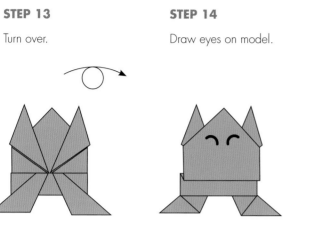

STEP 14

Draw eyes on model.

STEP 15

To make the frog jump, push down on the point, as shown, and then release.

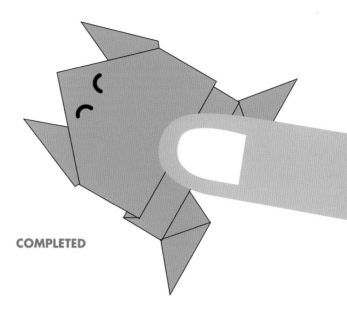

COMPLETED

SITTING LIKE A FROG

Frogs have a habit of sitting still. Whether using stillness as a strategy to avoid predators, waiting patiently to ambush flies with their tongue or just relaxing on a lily pad, it is common to see frogs just being still. This is not something that humans are particularly good at sometimes, especially in our busy, distracted modern world.

1. For this exercise, take some time to just *be*. You might like to go outside, and even sit near a pond or stream if possible. Being near water is extremely relaxing — just ask frogs. Even if you are inside, you can choose to just sit and let go of distractions. In some parts of the world you will find frogs in houses, usually in the shower or near the toilet, so we can safely assume it's possible to be still in any environment.

2. Check in with yourself. Is your mind busy? If it is, notice what needs to be let go of so you can just arrive fully in the present.

Inhabit your body fully, using it as an anchor to bring your attention back to whenever it wanders off.

3. Let go of any tension in your body. Find the most comfortable position possible and settle into that.

4. Notice what it's like to take some time to just *sit*. You don't need to treat this as a meditation session. Instead, just use it as an opportunity to practise sitting and being still.

5. It's inevitable that your mind will wander — perhaps quite a bit. It is impossible to stop that from happening, but you *can* get better at catching it. Just like a frog sitting on a lily pad waiting for a fly, simply sit in silence and observe what is happening. How long can you sit still for?

6. When you are ready, take a moment to notice the effect of simply taking some time to sit in stillness. Then mindfully hop off into whatever awaits you.

PINE TREE

Trees are symbols of nature and harmony. The 'tree of life' represents the interconnection of all life on the planet and can be found in the folklores of diverse cultures. Trees provide shelter to many animals and transform carbon dioxide into life-sustaining oxygen through their process of photosynthesis.

Pine trees are one of the most beloved of all trees. Their beauty lasts year-round and they are incredibly resilient, able to withstand both snow and withering heat. They are tall, representing objectivity and farsightedness. In certain religions, they signify divinity and new life.

The pine tree model can be used as a decoration during religious holidays. It is also extremely fun to fold.

HOW TO FOLD

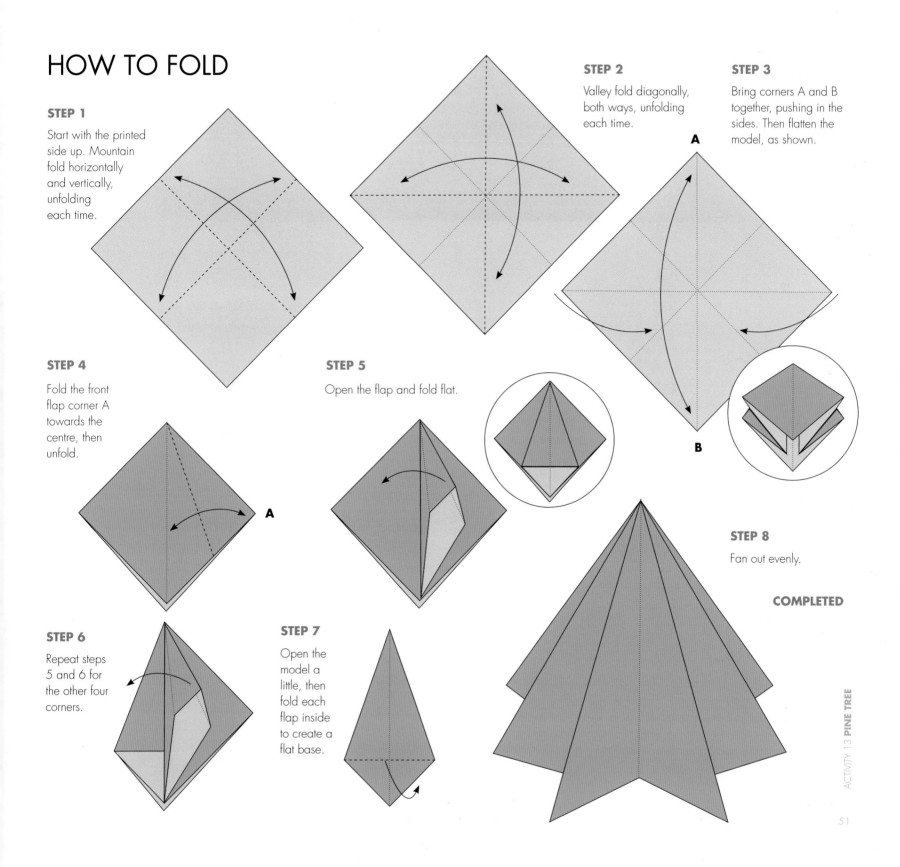

STEP 1

Start with the printed side up. Mountain fold horizontally and vertically, unfolding each time.

STEP 2

Valley fold diagonally, both ways, unfolding each time.

STEP 3

Bring corners A and B together, pushing in the sides. Then flatten the model, as shown.

A

B

STEP 4

Fold the front flap corner A towards the centre, then unfold.

A

STEP 5

Open the flap and fold flat.

STEP 6

Repeat steps 5 and 6 for the other four corners.

STEP 7

Open the model a little, then fold each flap inside to create a flat base.

STEP 8

Fan out evenly.

COMPLETED

STAND LIKE A TREE

Go outside and stand under a tree. It doesn't matter what kind of tree — just find one and take a moment to appreciate its beauty. Touch the strong trunk, feeling the texture of the bark and how it is solid yet flexible at the same time.

Notice the way the branches diverge from each other in complex patterns. Observe this right out to the tips of the branches. If the tree has leaves, notice their colour and texture, perhaps picking up a fallen one to observe it more closely. Notice the way the leaves provide shade and shelter for insects and animals. Listen to the rustle as the wind blows through them.

Look down and notice the roots. Some may be visible but most of them travel deep down into the ground beneath the tree. For many trees, the root system is the same size as the spread of the foliage. Take than in for a moment. Can you sense how deep the roots go, and how stable this makes the tree?

Great storms can come and go, and most trees remain firmly rooted in the earth, yet flexible enough in their trunk and branches to yield so that they can withstand even the strongest wind. Take a moment to reflect on that. Wouldn't that be a great way to be in the world? Well, guess what? You can!

Feel your own feet on the ground. Can you take your attention down into the ground beneath you and sense your own rootedness into the earth? How deep can you sense your roots going? Feel the strength of your trunk, your core. Allow it to be relaxed yet upright, with a straight spine. Notice how your body breathes when you stand in this upright, relaxed way. Notice what happens in your mind. What is the quality of your attention?

Feel your face and the top of our head. Notice how the wind and the sun, or maybe the rain, feels on your skin and in your hair. If you like, stretch your arms up and out, like branches reaching into the sky. Observe your mind as you do this.

Take a few more moments to experience the world the way a tree does. When you move off into your day, can you take some of this rooted, upright flexibility with you? How does this change your day? ■

LOTUS

The lotus flower is a symbol of purity. Its roots grow in mud but it blooms on top of the pond, representing transformation and awakening. It also represents spiritual awakening. Because of this, lotuses commonly feature in art and mythology in many countries, both Eastern and Western.

This beautiful model can be used by itself as decoration. It can even hold candles or be floated on water (if the paper is waxed first).

HOW TO FOLD

STEP 1

Start with the printed side down. Valley fold diagonally both ways, unfolding each time.

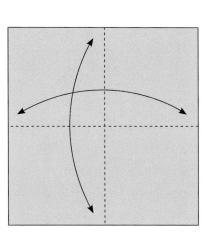

STEP 2

Fold each corner into the centre.

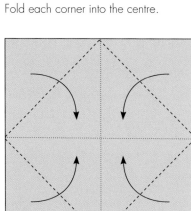

STEP 3

Fold in the corners again, as in step 2.

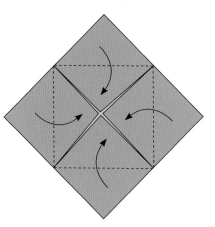

STEP 4

Flip model over.

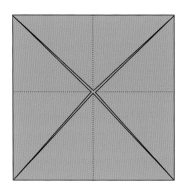

STEP 5

Fold each corner into the centre point again.

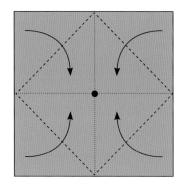

STEP 6

Fold top of corners down.

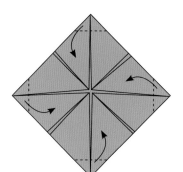

STEP 7

Flip model over.

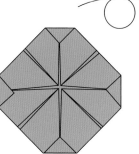

STEP 8

Carefully unfold all four sides, pulling each over to the other side until it pops up into a petal shape.

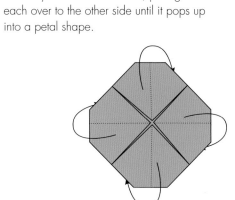

STEP 9

Repeat step 8 with the next layer to make more petals.

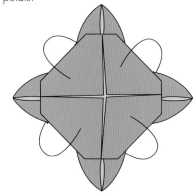

COMPLETED

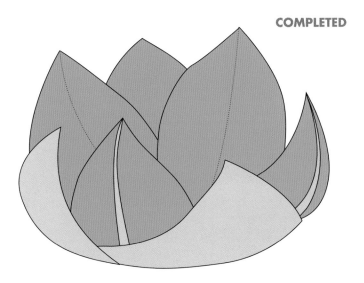

THE JEWEL IN THE LOTUS

As well as representing awakening, the lotus is a symbol of compassion. Compassion, like loving-kindness (which we learned how to cultivate on p. 36) is an important part of heartfulness. Loving-kindness simply means making the wish that all living beings enjoy happiness. Compassion is the willingness to hold the suffering of others in our heart rather than close ourselves off from it, and to do whatever we can to alleviate it.

Sometimes this means acting. This can be done in gentle ways, such as giving someone a hug. At times, compassion can be very direct and even wrathful, like a mother smacking her child's hand away from the power socket.

Sometimes, there may be nothing we can do directly, and all we can do is make the wish in our own mind for others to be happy and free from suffering. Even though this doesn't seem like much, it can powerfully transform our own mind and make us more loving and compassionate, which in turn deepens our mindfulness. We are more aware of our actions and so are spontaneously kinder to others. What began as simple wishes ripples out into the world.

Knowing when and how to respond to suffering takes great skill and requires the development of wisdom. For this reason, some wisdom traditions view full awakening as a coming together of compassion and wisdom.

Cultivating compassion and wisdom starts with being more mindful. This can be practised formally, through meditation, or informally, through everyday activities like the ones we have explored in this book.

To take this to the next level, you might like to experiment with starting your day by making the wish 'May all living beings be happy and free from suffering'. Repeat this to yourself a number of times, and return to it during the day. Also, if you witness suffering in others, what can you do to help? Even just making wishes for their happiness can be very powerful. ■

55

BOW

This is a very complicated model and will test all of the folding skills you have developed throughout the book. It is literally the bow on the present, and this is why I have put it last in the book. I strongly encourage you to practise your folding skills on simpler models before attempting this one.

It also presents a great opportunity to practise qualities of mindfulness such as focus, patience and self-compassion. These important qualities help us navigate the challenges that life throws up from time to time, and so folding this model is in many ways a microcosm of the reality of life. You may like to practise with regular paper before attempting the bow using the paper included in the book.

When completed, the bow is obviously a wonderful decoration. It can be affixed to presents, cards and letters. It could be used for wedding invitations or placeholders, and can even be worn as a brooch or hairpin. Before beginning, take a few moments to breathe and centre yourself in your body. Let go of any tension and any apprehension about folding this model. Challenges are best met with a calm, open mind.

HOW TO FOLD

STEP 1

Start with the printed side up. Mountain fold horizontally and vertically, unfolding each time.

STEP 2

Valley fold diagonally (both ways), unfolding each time.

STEP 3

Bring corners A and B together, pushing in the sides. Then flatten the model, as shown.

A

B

STEP 4

Valley fold the top corner down (1cm) along line shown then unfold.

STEP 5

Open model up again.

STEP 6

Re-crease the square valley folds into mountain folds by gently pinching up. Take your time with this. Now re-fold the sides as you did in step 3 and push in the top, as shown. Flatten the model.

STEP 7

Valley fold the top-left and top-right edges, as shown (front layer only). Flip the model over.

STEP 8

Repeat step 7 on the other side.

STEP 9

Gently open the model without unfolding the centre square. Flatten the square, then flip the model over.

STEP 10

Now we need to cheat a little (traditional origami discourages cutting, but sometimes it's good to break the rules a bit to make sure our mind stays flexible). Carefully cut along the four folds, as shown, until you reach the inner corner of each fold.

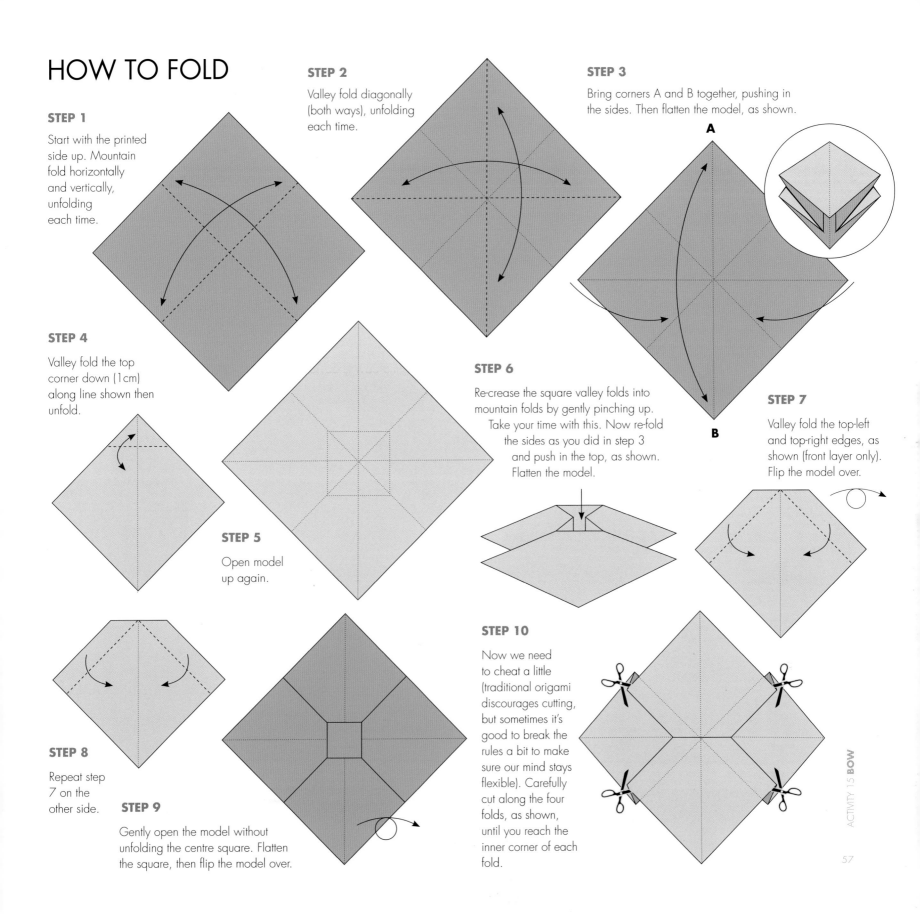

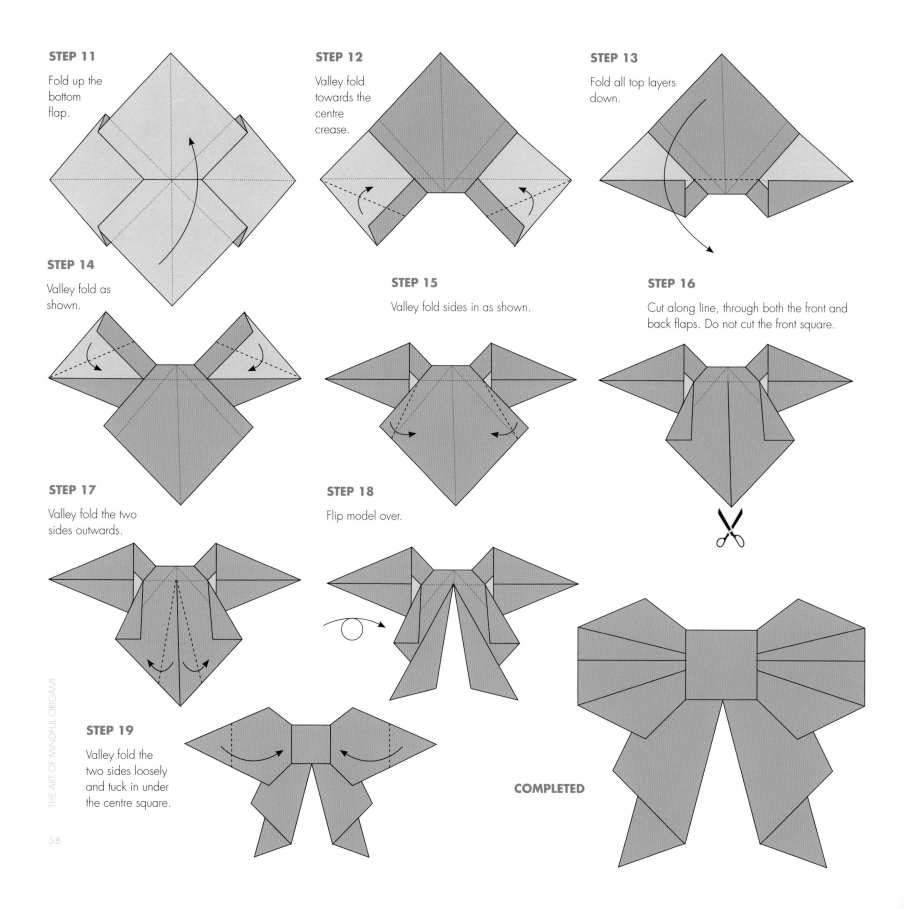

STEP 11

Fold up the bottom flap.

STEP 12

Valley fold towards the centre crease.

STEP 13

Fold all top layers down.

STEP 14

Valley fold as shown.

STEP 15

Valley fold sides in as shown.

STEP 16

Cut along line, through both the front and back flaps. Do not cut the front square.

STEP 17

Valley fold the two sides outwards.

STEP 18

Flip model over.

STEP 19

Valley fold the two sides loosely and tuck in under the centre square.

COMPLETED

THE GIFT OF PRESENCE

On page 16 we saw how good it feels to give. Research shows that generosity has wonderful benefits for physical and mental health. In fact, when we really pay attention we find that giving makes us much happier than receiving.

But here's a question: is it giving people *gifts* that makes you happy, or could it be enough just to give them *presence*?

You may already know the answer to this from your own experience. If not, here is a simple experiment to find out (mindfulness gives us the tools to experiment and learn from our direct experiences, which is always the most powerful kind of learning):

1. Think of someone you love.

2. Go and spend some time with them.

3. Really *be* with them.

This means bringing your full awareness to them, listening intently to what they are saying. Doing so requires cultivating an attitude of 'beginner's mind', being genuinely open to and interested in what they are saying, rather than offering advice or just 'reloading' and waiting for your turn to speak.

It also involves enjoying the moments of silence, just sitting and being near them. Enjoy the moment together. Let your presence and engagement be an invitation for them to engage with the world in the same way. And then let their engagement deepen yours.

Be playful, exploring new possibilities and new things. Go and do something new that neither of you have ever done before. Do this as much as you can. Notice the effect on your life and relationships. Presence is the greatest gift you can give anyone, including yourself. ■

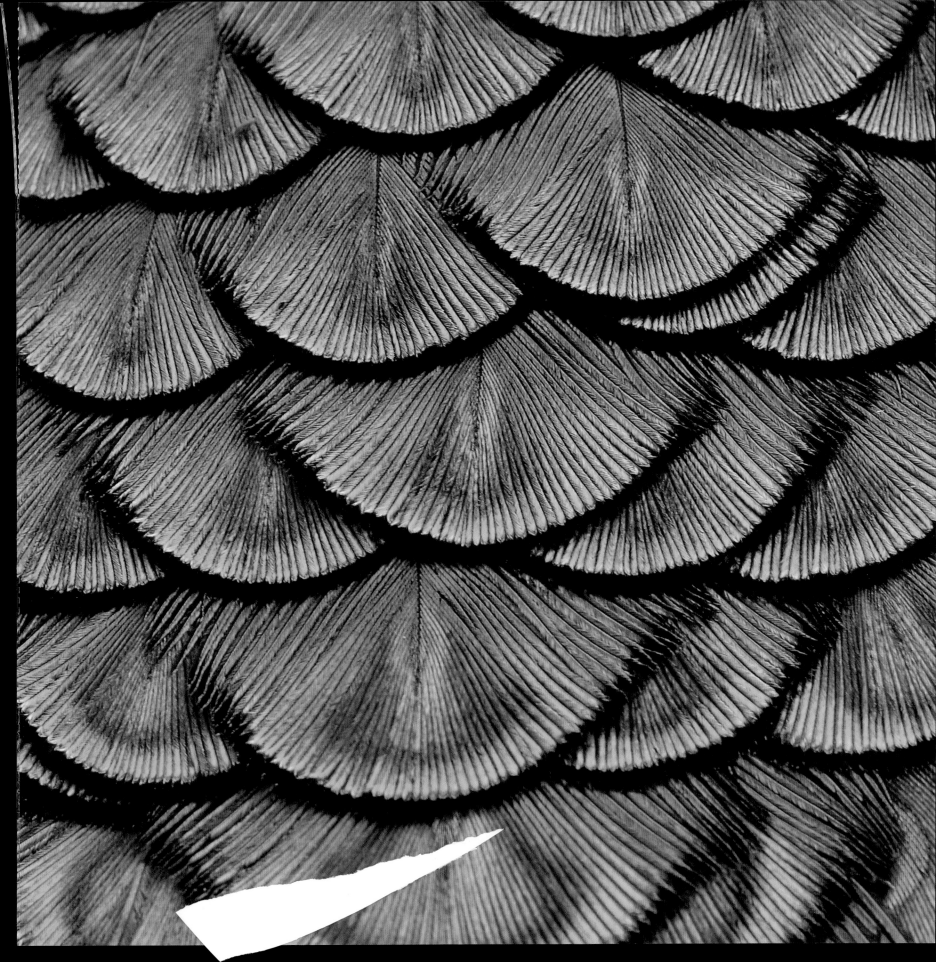

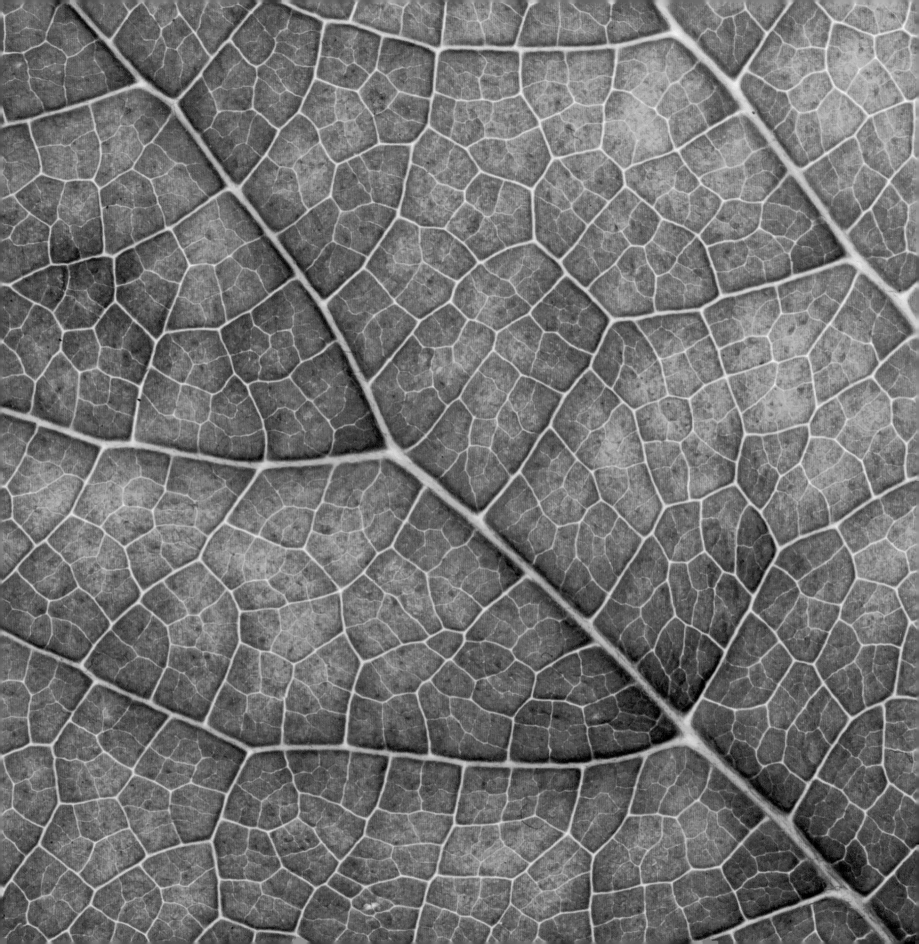

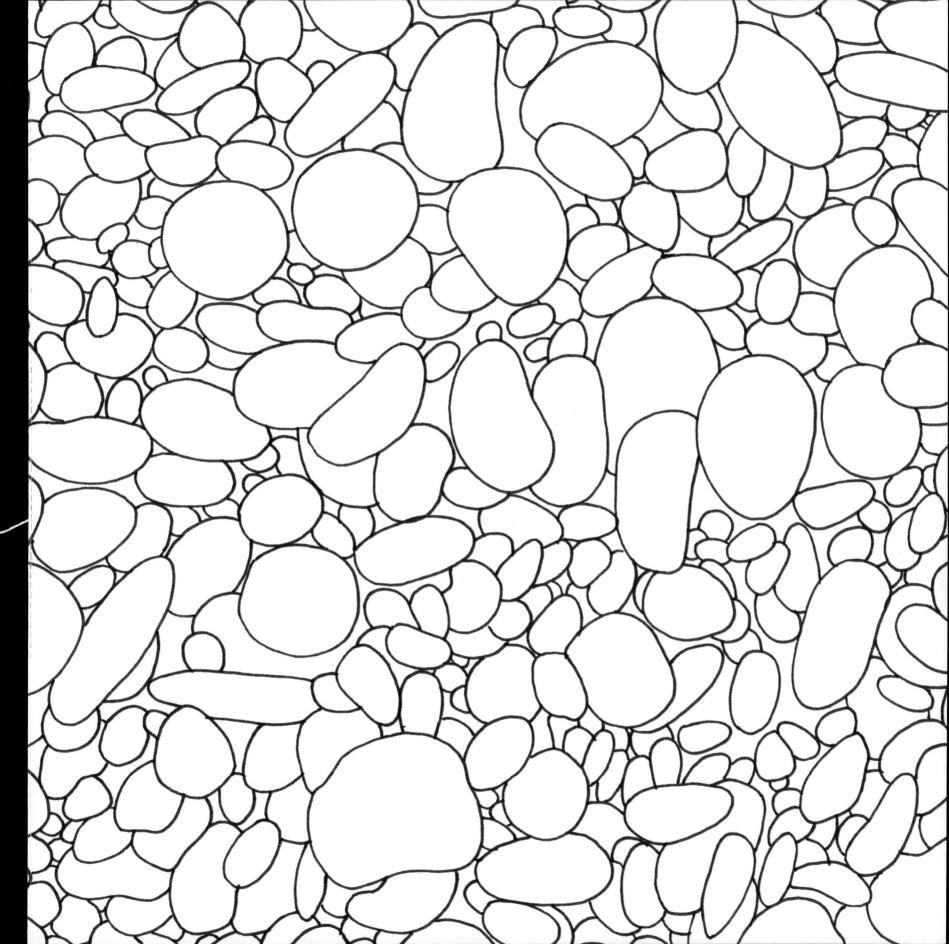

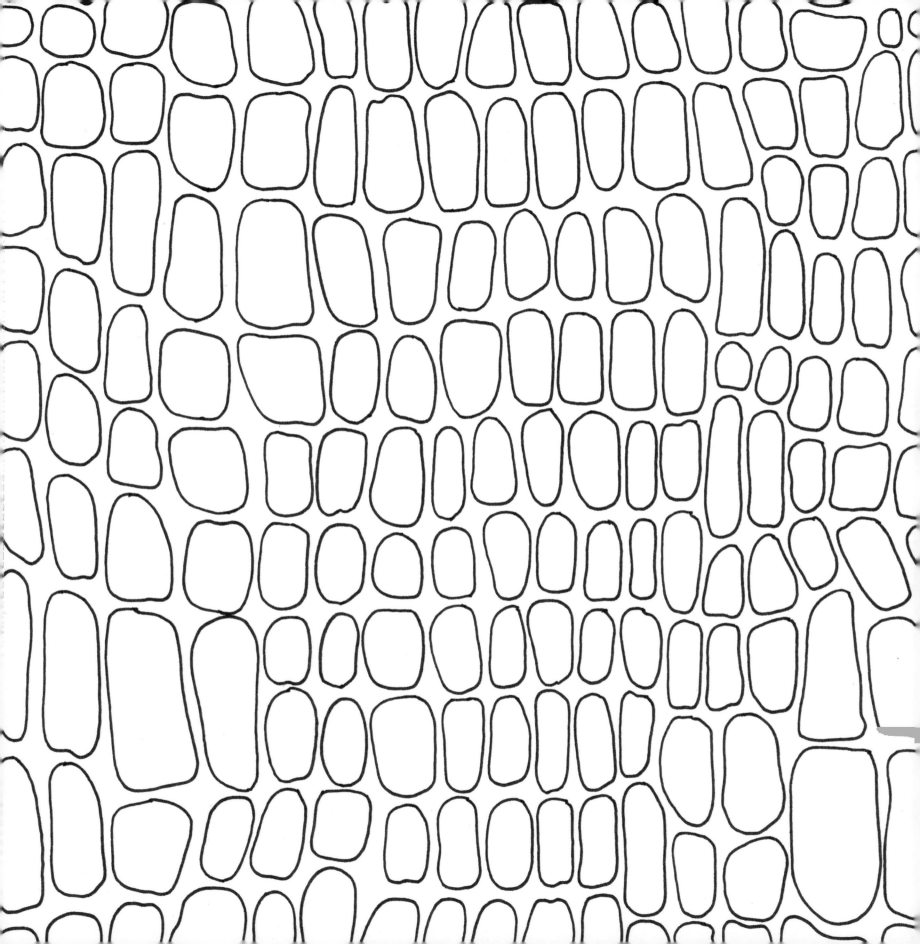